St Paul's
THE CATHEDRAL GUIDE

The Ground Floor

The great West Door of the cathedral is open only on special occasions, so visitors enter by the doors to the left and the right. We shall go in through the door on the left – the North West Door.

Almost immediately on entering there are two chapels, the first of which is **All Souls' Chapel***. This was dedicated in 1925 to the memory of Field Marshal Earl Kitchener of Khartoum (d. 1916) and all others who were killed during the war 1914–1918.

The recumbent effigy of Lord Kitchener, the Pietà (the figure of the dead Christ supported by the Virgin Mary) above the altar, the St Michael and St George figures, were all sculpted by the Scottish artist Sir William Reid Dick (d. 1961). It was Reid Dick who, after the Second World War, was responsible for the bronze statue of President Franklin Roosevelt in Grosvenor Square.

In a recess in the north wall of the chapel, behind a gilt grille, there are Rolls of Honour of the Royal Engineers who died in the First and Second World Wars. The large, silver candlesticks were the gift of the London Rifle Brigade and were made from cups and trophies won by Brigade members. Outside, on the wall opposite the chapel, hang the colours of the Grenadier Guards, deposited in 1938.

A few steps further along is the larger of these two chapels – the **Chapel of St Dunstan***. The screen at the entrance is by Jonathan Maine, one of the highly gifted carvers employed by Sir Christopher Wren. The chandelier is dated 1778 and was formerly in the church of St Mildred,

---

Areas marked with an asterisk (*) may be viewed only when accompanied by a Guide. (See page 2 for details of tours.)

ABOVE: *The Chapel of St Dunstan. The hangings behind the altar were the gift of the Friends of St Paul's.*

RIGHT: *Effigy of Field Marshal Earl Kitchener of Khartoum (1850–1916). He served in the Sudan, South Africa and India. In August 1914 he was appointed Secretary for War and was drowned when H.M.S. Hampshire was sunk off Orkney in 1916.*

FACING PAGE: *St Paul's from the south-east, a view that conveys the supreme majesty of Wren's great dome. The stone tower on the right is all that remains of an oblong Wren church, St Augustine-with-St Faith, which was built in 1680–87 and bombed during an air raid in 1941. Wren carefully related the steeple of his church to St Paul's, forming a light contrast with the massiveness of the dome.*

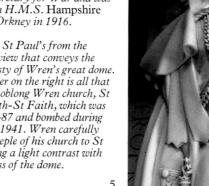

Poultry, which was demolished in 1872. The mosaics at the east end of the chapel are the first to be done in the cathedral by Sir William Richmond (d. 1921) who later decorated the choir and the aisles. The mosaic at the west end, portraying the women at the Sepulchre, is the work of the Venetian artist Antonio Salviati (d. 1890).

Continuing down the **North Aisle**, the memorial under the first window is to Lord Leighton (d. 1896) the painter and sculptor, who was elected President of the Royal Academy in 1878. He was raised to the peerage on 24 January 1896 – the day before he died.

Next, on the right, stands the great monument to the Duke of Wellington (d. 1852). The artist, Alfred Stevens, worked on this monument for twenty years until his death in 1875. The bronze figures, on either side above the columns, represent 'Virtue keeping Vice beneath its feet' and 'Truth plucking out the tongue of Calumny'. The figure of the Duke on horseback was not added until 1912. The choice of the sculptor John Tweed (d. 1933)

to create this from Stevens's sketch model caused much controversy.

Just past the Wellington monument is the memorial to the Indian Army (1746–1947); and on the opposite side of the aisle there is the monument of General Gordon, who was killed defending Khartoum, with the colours of the Royal Fusiliers hanging above it. These regimental colours were received in the cathedral on 14 December 1897.

Further down on the left we come to a realistic, mock double-door, guarded by two stone angels. This is the memorial to Lord Melbourne (d. 1848) who was Prime Minister from 1833 to 1841. The inscription reads: 'Through the Gate of Death we pass to our Joyful Resurrection'.

We are now at the eastern end of the North Aisle. On both sides there are tablets listing the Deans of St Paul's from 1066 to date. On the left side is the door to the Lord Mayor's Vestry, and then the statue of Sir Joshua Reynolds (d. 1792) the portrait painter and first President of the Royal Academy.

Now, turning left into the restored

North Transept, which was severely damaged by a bomb on the night of 16/17 April 1941, we see the life-size Virgin and Child sculpted in terra-cotta. This is the work of the Portuguese-born artist, Josephena de Vasconcellos, who lives at Ambleside in the Lake District. Beyond the statue is the massive marble font which was made in 1726–7 by Francis Bird (d. 1731). Some twenty years earlier, Bird had been responsible for the pediment over the west portico depicting the Conversion of St Paul, and for the figures at the top – St Paul flanked by St Peter and St James, with the four evangelists on the towers.

The font is in the **North Transept Chapel**, often referred to as the 'Middlesex Chapel', *set apart for private prayer*. The colours of the Middlesex Regiment hang in the chapel and the chairs and kneelers are memorial gifts from the regiment. The painting behind the altar, of the School of Titian, depicts the Virgin and Child with St Luke.

In the north wall of the chapel there is an aumbry (or recess) for the reservation of the Blessed Sacrament,

the door of which was carved in 1979 by the present Cathedral Master Carver, Tony Webb. The decoration is a representation of a 'Pelican in her Piety'. This fable of the pelican reviving or feeding her young with her own blood, was recounted by the Norfolk poet and priest John Skelton (d. 1529) in his 'Armoury of Birdis', thus:

> Than sayd the Pellycane,
> When my birdis be slayne
> With my bloude I them revyve.
> Scrypture doth record,
> The same dyd our Lord,
> And rose from deth to lyve.

We leave the North Transept Chapel, with the North Door behind us, and pass the monuments to General Thomas Dundas (d. 1794) on our left and Captain Robert Faulknor, R.N. (d. 1795) on our right. Turning left towards the **North Choir Aisle** (also known as the Minor Canons' Aisle) we see at the entrance the statue of Samuel Johnson (d. 1784) the great English lexicographer, man of letters and conversationalist, surprisingly attired as an Ancient Greek.

The way into the aisle is through the iron gates made by Jean Tijou (d. 1712?). Most of the ironwork in the cathedral was done by this superb French craftsman during the eighteen years up to 1708 that he was employed by Wren at St Paul's. The ceilings of this aisle and the South Choir Aisle are decorated with mosaics.. by Richmond.

The first door on the left in the aisle leads to the Minor Canons' Vestry. Opposite to this, the door inscribed 'Organista' used to give access to the organ console when it was situated at this north side of the Choir. The carved wood panelling, also on the right, is the rear of the north side of the choir stalls and is by Grinling Gibbons (d. 1720). Gibbons was born in Rotterdam (see *Dictionary of National Biography*). He was discovered working at Deptford by the diarist John Evelyn, who recommended him to Wren. The inset iron panels are by Tijou.

On the left is the Music Library and then a Memorial Screen listing the names of former choristers who died in the two World Wars. Further down the aisle, on the right, is the splendid Sanctuary Screen with gates, by Tijou. The date at the top, 1890, is the year when this screen and the one in the South Choir Aisle were re-erected, having formerly been across the west end of the Choir.

FACING PAGE LEFT: *The charming life-size terracotta sculpture of the Virgin and Child. Made originally in plaster for the Nativity scene in 1960, this version was presented to the cathedral by Bernard Sunley.*

FACING PAGE RIGHT: *The North Transept ('Middlesex') Chapel. In the foreground is the marble font made by Francis Bird in 1726–7. The altar, seen in the background, was made in* 1973 and is dedicated to the memory of Bernard Spink who was a priest in the London diocese for 38 years.

ABOVE: *The enormous monument to the Duke of Wellington (1769–1852) which occupies one of the bays on the north side of the Nave. Some 48 of Wellington's battles are listed around the base. The recumbent figure of the Duke is almost out of sight on top of a marble sarcophagus.*

7

The Chapel of the Modern Martyrs, at the east end of the aisle, commemorates Anglican martyrs since 1850. It was dedicated in 1961 and all the known names are recorded in a book secured in a glass-topped, marble casket. The altar was previously in the Jesus Chapel and the Crucifix was part of the reredos of 1880 which was damaged by a bomb on the night of 9/10 October 1940 and subsequently removed.

Turning right, through the Sanctuary Screen gate, into the east end apse behind the High Altar, we come to the **American Memorial Chapel.** This was formerly the Jesus Chapel, which also was damaged by the bomb of October 1940. The costs of constructing and decorating this chapel were met by subscriptions from the British people. The Roll of Honour was presented to the cathedral on Independence Day 1951 by General Eisenhower. It lists the 28,000 American citizens, based in Britain, who died during the Second World War; and it lies open, in a case of glass and gold, on a marble pedestal.

The wall-panelling, the stalls and the borders of the three windows, are rich in American symbols and insignia. At the ends of the stalls there are medallion portraits of Queen

★

ABOVE LEFT: *Detail from the gate in the Sanctuary screen on the south side. When this screen was moved from the west end of the Choir in 1890 some additions to Tijou's work were wrought at Lamberhurst by Messrs Barketin and Krall from designs by Bodley and Garner.*

BELOW LEFT: *The Roll of Honour was designed by the artist-designer Trygve A. Revelstad and bound by Messrs Sangorski and Sutcliffe of London under the direction of Stanley Bray. It was presented to the cathedral by General Eisenhower in 1951.*

FACING PAGE: *The American Memorial Chapel contains many examples of the finest British craftsmanship. The silver-gilt cross and candlesticks are hand-hammered and were made by the London firm of D. & J. Welby. Wainwright & Waring of Mortlake produced the wrought-iron altar rails to match the existing Tijou gates. The three tall, stained-glass windows were designed by Brian Thomas to represent the Service, Sacrifice and Resurrection of the faithful soldier.*

8

Elizabeth and President Eisenhower, and of the two architects of the chapel – S. E. Dykes Bower and Godfrey Allen. The dedication of the chapel by Henry Campbell, Bishop of London, took place on 26 November 1958 in the presence of Her Majesty Queen Elizabeth and Vice-President Richard Nixon.

We now move into the **Lady Chapel**, at the east end of the **South Choir Aisle.** Wren made no provision for a Lady Chapel and this one was completed as recently as 1959. The oak altar table is Wren's original High Altar and the Victorian statue of the Blessed Virgin was part of the 1880 reredos. It is now set here in a section of Wren's organ screen which was taken down in 1858.

The wooden crucifix and candlesticks on the altar are of 18th-century Bavarian make and were presented to St Paul's in October 1958 by the President of West Germany, Theodor Heuss, during his state visit to this country.

Continuing along the South Choir Aisle, the memorial to Bishop Blomfield (d. 1857) is on the left. As Bishop of London, Charles Blomfield carried out a remarkable programme of church-building and, during the twenty-nine years of his episcopate, he consecrated more than 200 new churches.

Next on the left, in a niche, stands the figure of John Donne (d. 1631) the most famous Dean of St Paul's. This effigy of Donne dressed in a shroud, was sculpted by Nicholas Stone the elder (d. 1647) from a drawing previously made and kept at Donne's bedside during the last weeks of his life. It is the only complete statue from Old St Paul's to have survived the Great Fire. In his later years, as T. S. Eliot (d. 1965) wrote of the

★

ABOVE LEFT: *The Lady Chapel, which was created in 1959. The photograph shows Wren's original high altar and part of his organ screen framing the Virgin and Child. On the right is the Diocesan banner of the Mothers' Union. The altar ornaments were gifts from West Germany.*

LEFT: *Part of the monument to Captain George Westcott (1743–1798). The carvings around the base of the monument include Egyptian imagery and also naval engagements commemorating Westcott's death during the Battle of the Nile.*

ERECTED AT THE PUBLIC EXPENSE, TO THE MEMORY OF
GEORGE BLAGDON WESTCOTT,
CAPTAIN OF THE MAJESTIC;
WHO, AFTER THIRTY-THREE YEARS OF MERITORIOUS SERVICE, FELL GLORIOUSLY
IN THE VICTORY OBTAINED OVER THE FRENCH FLEET OFF ABOUKIR, THE FIRST DAY OF AUGUST, IN THE YEAR MDCCXCVIII. IN THE FORTY-SIXTH YEAR OF HIS AGE.

Jacobean dramatist John Webster, Donne 'was much possessed by death, and saw the skull beneath the skin'. But he had no fear of it, as the opening and closing lines of his defiant sonnet 'To Death' testify:

Death be not proud, though some
   have callèd thee
Mighty and dreadful, for thou art
   not so . . .
One short sleep past, we wake
   eternally,
And Death shall be no more:
   Death, thou shalt die!

An interesting curiosity appears at the side of this memorial, affixed to the wall. It is a piece of stone from Solomon's Temple at Jerusalem. This was given by the art historian Sir James Fergusson to Sir James Penne-thorne. The latter's daughter, Anna Liddon, passed it on to the cathedral in 1889. Another piece is fixed to the wall a little further on, past the Prebendaries' Vestry door.

On the right, there is the striking statue of Bishop Mandell Creighton (d. 1901) the ecclesiastical historian. The panelling on this side, as in the North Choir Aisle, is by Gibbons. The door on the left is to the Dean's Vestry.

We now leave the South Choir Aisle. Immediately through the gates, the statue of John Howard (d. 1790), the prison reformer, stands on the left. This was the first monument to be placed in the present cathedral and, ironically, Howard was a Quaker. Turning left into the **South Transept**, the memorial tablet on the wall is to Captain Scott and the members of his expedition who died on the return journey from the South Pole in 1912.

★

RIGHT: *A detail of the full-length effigy of John Donne, poet and priest (1573–1631), Dean of St Paul's from 1621 to 1631. At the top of the monument are the Arms of the Dean and Chapter and Donne's Arms combined. This monument was the only one to survive the Great Fire intact.*

John Donne wrote his own epitaph, which he concluded by declaring he was 'Looking towards Him whose name is the Resurrection'. His sermons rank among the best of the 17th century, and his 'metaphysical' poems are still popular today.

The entrance to the Crypt (to which we shall return later) is next on the left and opposite it is the statue of Sir Henry Lawrence (d. 1857) who was fatally wounded at the siege of Lucknow during the Indian Mutiny.

The South Transept has a great number of memorials, not all of which will be mentioned here. On our left is the monument of Admiral Earl Howe (d. 1799) who settled the naval mutiny at Spithead in 1797; and, facing us, that of Admiral Lord Collingwood, second-in-command at the battle of Trafalgar.

Bearing round, we see on the left the memorial to one of the greatest of English painters, J. M. W. Turner (d. 1851) who willed a large collection of his pictures to the nation. Opposite, is the statue of General Lord Heathfield (d. 1790), who successfully defended Gibraltar against the forces of Spain and France from 1779 until 1783. Also on this side are the statues of General Lord Cornwallis (d. 1805), who surrendered to Washington at Yorktown in 1781; and Admiral Lord Nelson (d. 1805), whose tomb is in the Crypt.

In this area of the South Transept hang the Banners of the Dominions – Australia, New Zealand and Canada – alongside the Royal Banner and the Banner of the United Kingdom. They were placed here by the Dean

and Chapter in 1935 to commemorate the Silver Jubilee of His Majesty King George V.

On the left is the memorial to General Sir John Moore (d. 1809) who was killed, during the Peninsular War, at the battle of Corunna and was buried there. He was further commemorated by the Irish poet Charles Wolfe (d. 1823) in 'The Burial of Sir John Moore after Corunna', which begins: 'Not a drum was heard, not a funeral note, as his corpse to the rampart we hurried . . .'

We are now facing the memorial to the Scottish general Sir Ralph Abercromby (d. 1801) who was mortally wounded leading his troops against the French at Alexandria. To the left of Abercromby stands the memorial to Sir Astley Cooper (d. 1841) surgeon to George IV.

Bearing right, we come to the monuments of Admiral Lord Lyons (d. 1858) on the left and Dr William Babington (d. 1833) physician to Guy's Hospital and founder of the Geological Society, on the right. A little further along the same side, in a niche, is the Roll of Honour of the members of the Merchant Navy and the Fishing Fleets who died serving in the Second World War.

As we turn left into the **South Aisle**, the statue of Sir William Jones (d. 1794) is at the corner. Jones was a

lawyer, poet, linguist and Oriental scholar and the statue carries many symbolic references to Western and Oriental mythology. He died in Calcutta, where he was a High Court Judge, and the directors of the East India Company voted the money for this monument.

On the left are the stairs to the Whispering Gallery and the Dome. There are tablets here, on both sides of the aisle, listing the Bishops of London from the year 314.

The monuments on the left of the South Aisle include those to Captain George Westcott (d. 1798) killed while in command of H.M.S. *Majestic* at the battle of the Nile; Thomas Middleton (d. 1822) the first Protestant Bishop of India; and Captain Rundell Burges (d. 1797) who died on board his ship *Ardent* fighting the Dutch at the battle of Camperdown south of the Texel.

On the right, almost opposite the Middleton monument, is William Holman Hunt's picture *The Light of the World*. Holman Hunt (d. 1910) was one of the 'Pre-Raphaelite Brotherhood' and he painted two versions of this picture of Christ knocking at a door. The first, which was completed in 1854, is in Keble College, Oxford; this version was not painted until 1900.

Next on the right, in a bay, is the small movable organ, sometimes called 'Willis on Wheels'. It was made in 1881 by Henry Willis (d. 1901) and was rebuilt by Noel Mander in 1970. In several emergencies, it has been used for full cathedral services.

Towards the end of the aisle, on the left, is the **Chapel of the Order of St Michael and St George***. This

Continued on page 16

★

ABOVE LEFT: *This chapel in the South Aisle became the spiritual centre of the Order of St Michael and St George in 1906.*

LEFT: *The splendid geometrical staircase in the south-west corner of the cathedral. The door which can be seen at the top leads to the Library Aisle, at the triforium level. Above this area, there is the clock tower.*

FACING PAGE: *The magnificent view of the Nave from the vestibule. In the foreground, on the right, is the organ on wheels. The runs of arches and saucer domes draw the eye eastwards to the High Altar and the superb stained-glass windows of the American Memorial Chapel beyond.*

FACING PAGE: *The Dome of St Paul's, for nearly 300 years the most famous City of London landmark. It still rises above the post-war, high-rise buildings. The height to the top of the cross from the churchyard pavement is 365 feet. The original ball and cross were replaced by the present structure in 1821.*

The sectional drawing of the dome: A is the outer dome of timber, lead-sheathed; B the brick cone which supports the lantern; C the inner dome of brick; D lantern and ball and cross; and E two stainless steel girdles.

The photograph of the interior of the dome shows the windows and pilasters, with niches at intervals accommodating statues of Doctors of the Church. Above are the Thornhill frescos.

ABOVE: *The Whispering Gallery, which derives its name from the fact that a whisper at one side can be clearly heard at the opposite side – over 100 feet away. The gallery is also the best place from which to view the Thornhill paintings in the dome.*

RIGHT: *Sir James Thornhill was appointed in 1715 to decorate the dome. This is one of his eight monochrome frescos, depicting incidents in the life of St Paul.*

15

has been, in turn, the Consistory Court of the Bishop of London, the place where the Wellington Monument was housed, and the Baptistry. In 1906 it was dedicated to its present use.

The Order was instituted in 1818 and its honours are conferred for distinguished services to the Commonwealth. The Anniversary Services are held in the cathedral in July.

At the entrance is a screen by Jonathan Maine, but the internal fitments and decoration are of this century. Over the teak stalls hang the banners of the Knights Grand Cross of the Order. The figure of St George is above the altar and the Prelate's Throne is to the left of it. Opposite the altar are the Royal Seats.

The last door on the left of the South Aisle leads to the **Geometrical Staircase***. This is a spiral of 92 stone steps – and an iron balustrade by Tijou – with no newel support. The steps are embedded only a few inches into the wall on the right-hand side, but the weight of each step is taken by the one immediately below it, and so on down to the stone floor.

Near this last door there are memorials to the men of the Coldstream Guards who died in the Crimean and South African wars. We now turn back and cross northwards towards the Nave.

At the entrance to the **Nave**, a memorial is set in the floor. This is to the members of 'St Paul's Watch', the group of volunteers who kept watch in the cathedral during air-raids from 1939 to 1945 and, in the words of the memorial, 'by the Grace of God saved this Cathedral from destruction'. Looking eastwards from this position, we have an uninterrupted view of the remainder of our ground floor tour: straight down the Nave, through the Dome area and the Choir, to the High Altar.

The Nave, 40 feet wide and 89 feet high, consists of four bays on either side. All along, over the bay arches, runs a cornice above which is the iron railing of the **Triforium**, or gallery. Above the triforium is a clerestory (row of windows) of plain glass. The ceiling of the Nave has transverse arches and four saucer-shaped domes. At the eastern end of the Nave we come to the area under the great **Dome.**

The weight of the Dome and its superstructure is 64,000 tons and this is supported by the eight piers. These were strengthened during the extensive repair and restoration of the Dome in 1925–1930.

The four Quarter Domes are decorated with mosaics by Sir William Richmond. The events they depict are: (N.E.) Our Lord enthroned on the Cross; (N.W.) the Appearance of Our Lord, sometimes called the Commission to St Paul; (S.W.) the Entombment; (S.E.) the Ascension.

The mosaics in the spandrels under the Whispering Gallery depict the four Evangelists – Matthew, Mark, Luke and John – and the prophets Isaiah, Jeremiah, Ezekiel and Daniel. All these are the work of Salviati.

Above the **Whispering Gallery** are the Dome windows and pilasters with niches at intervals. In these niches there are statues of eight great Doctors of the Church, early Christian Fathers distinguished for their learning and sanctity. They are the Saints Ambrose, Augustine, Jerome and Gregory, of the Western Church; Athanasius, Basil, Gregory of Nazianzus and Chrysostom, of the Eastern Church.

The inner dome, above, is decorated with Sir James Thornhill's frescos of incidents in the life of St Paul.

In the black-and-white marble paving under the Dome, is the memorial to Sir Winston Churchill (d. 1965) marking the place where the catafalque stood during his State Funeral. Sir Winston is buried at Bladon, near Blenheim Palace.

From this position we are best able to see the west faces of the arches enclosing the saucer domes of the

★

FACING PAGE ABOVE: *The Choir ceiling saucer domes, decorated with mosaics by Sir William Richmond between 1892 and 1895.*

FACING PAGE BELOW: *A detail from the westernmost saucer dome in the Choir portraying the creation of beasts. All kinds of animals are shown and sections are divided by palm trees.*

ABOVE RIGHT: *A view of the Grinling Gibbons carvings on the organ case situated on the south wall of the Choir.*

RIGHT: *Part of the marble paving under the dome where Sir Christopher Wren's epitaph is repeated (shown in full on page 22). A translation of it ends, 'If you seek his monument, look around you.'*

17

Choir ceiling. The inscriptions read: *Benedicite omnia opera Domini Domino* (O all ye works of the Lord, bless ye the Lord); *Omnes bestiae et pecora* (All beasts and cattle); *Omnia quae moventur in aquis* (All things that move in the waters); *Omnes volucres coeli* (All fowls of the air). The last three inscriptions indicate the contents of the decorated saucer domes by Richmond – animals in the first one, fish in the next and birds in the last one nearest the Altar.

In front of the Choir, on the left, is the brass eagle Lectern on a pedestal supported by four lions. It was made by the founder Jacob Sutton, in 1719. On the right is the Pulpit. This was commissioned by the Friends of St Paul's to mark the 250th anniversary of the completion of the cathedral in 1710 and it was dedicated four years later by the Bishop of London, Robert Stopford, at the Festival Service of the Friends of St Paul's. It was designed by the then Surveyor to the Fabric, Lord Mottistone (d. 1963). The canopy is not only in keeping with the style of the pulpits of Wren's time, but also improves the acoustics. The funds for the canopy were provided by the Chapel Committee of the Order of the British Empire. The crucifix, a memorial to Lord Mottistone, is the work of the sculptor E. J. C. Russell.

The Organ is in two parts situated on the north and south walls at the entrance to the Choir, with the console to the east of the organ on the south wall. It was built in 1694–1697 by Bernard Smith and the case was made by Charles Hopson and carved by Grinling Gibbons. The organ was divided and rebuilt in its present positions by Henry Willis in 1872. After being damaged during the Second World War it was taken down and stored. From 1973–1977 it underwent a major reconstruction by Noel Mander and an additional section was placed on the south west

★

ABOVE LEFT: *Chairs and kneelers reserved at St Paul's for use by Her Majesty The Queen and other members of the Royal Family.*

LEFT: *Part of the Grinling Gibbons decorative carving at the back of the north side of the choir stalls, restored by the cathedral's Master Carver.*

FACING PAGE: *A view of the High Altar with the American Memorial Chapel at the back.*

end of the Triforium to counter the time lag. Also at this time the new Royal Trumpets, which can be seen projecting from the west gallery, were installed.

We now enter the **Choir***. The first stall on the south side is the Dean's stall; opposite is the stall of the Archdeacon of London. Next to these are the stalls of the Canons Residentiary and the Minor Canons. Midway down the south side is the stall belonging to the Bishop of London, which he occupies on unofficial occasions; opposite this is the Lord Mayor's stall. The Bishop's Throne, or *cathedra*, is at the east end of the south side. (The principal church of a diocese contains the

bishop's *cathedra* and thus it is called the 'cathedral' church.)

The other stalls are allocated to the Bishops Suffragan and Archdeacons of the diocese, and the 30 Prebendaries of St Paul's. Over the back of a prebendary stall appears the name of the 'prebend' or estate (e.g. Brondesbury, Sneating, Willesden) which formerly provided an income for the occupant. The Latin words beneath each place-name are the opening phrase of the particular section of the psalms which that prebendary recites daily. The carvings in the chóir stalls, including the splendid pieces on the pillars at the sides of the *cathedra*, are the work of Grinling Gibbons.

Appropriately, our ground floor tour ends at the **High Altar***. This altar, consecrated in May 1958, replaced the High Altar and Reredos of 1888 which were damaged by the bomb which struck the east end of the cathedral in October 1940. It is a memorial to the people of the Commonwealth who died serving in the two World Wars.

The Altar is Italian marble and the cross and candlesticks are gilt bronze. The stones in the middle of the cross are amethyst and polished rock crystal. These ornaments were the gift of the Goldsmiths' Company.

The great baldacchino, or canopy over the Altar, is made of English oak. Christ Triumphant stands on top.

19

The Crypt

The Crypt of St Paul's is unusual in that it extends under the whole building, rather than being confined to the chancel, or eastern end. The enormous weight of the cathedral is supported by the great pillars which are seen here. The Crypt contains many memorials and graves (though burials no longer take place), two chapels, Wren's Great Model and a Treasury. There is space in this guide only to mention items and areas of interest, and to give a brief introduction to the most important ones.

In the south-east corner, which is reached by turning right at the bottom of the steps to the Crypt, lies the plain, marble slab marking the grave of Sir Christopher Wren (d. 1723). On the wall above, is the famous Latin inscription which suggests that those seeking his monument should look around them – implying that St Paul's itself is Wren's monument.

At the east end is the **Chapel of the Order of the British Empire.** This is St Faith's Chapel, dedicated in 1960 to the Order of the British Empire which was founded in 1917. Men and women are appointed to the Order, for distinguished services to the country, as Knights (G.B.E. or K.B.E.), Dames (D.B.E.),

Commanders (C.B.E.), Officers (O.B.E.) or Members (M.B.E.). Services connected with those belonging to the Order are frequently held in the chapel, including baptisms and weddings.

To the left, in the north-east corner, is **St Christopher's Chapel**, which is the children's chapel and is used by many visiting groups. Above the altar is a stained-glass panel depicting the saint carrying the Christ-child.

The middle area of the Crypt is occupied by the massive tombs of the Duke of Wellington (d. 1852) and Admiral Lord Nelson (d. 1805). Surrounding these, are the tombs and memorials of many other military and naval leaders.

Continuing westward, past Nelson's tomb, we come to Wren's Great Model, his second design for the new cathedral, which was rejected. After being on loan to the South Kensington Museum, the Great Model was for many years on the Triforium of the cathedral and later in the Trophy Room. It was refurbished and re-erected here in the Crypt in 1982, to commemorate the 350th anniversary of the birth of Christopher Wren. This design formed the basis of the present St

Paul's, not the one which was officially accepted – the Warrant Design. This latter design has been variously described as 'fantastic' and 'a nightmare'.

To the north of Nelson's tomb there is the **Treasury**, which was opened in 1981. Here are displayed church and secular plate, liturgical vestments and other embroideries, belonging to St Paul's and churches throughout the Diocese of London.

In all parts of the Crypt there are memorials to artists, musicians, statesmen, writers and, of course, church dignitaries connected with St Paul's. William Ralph Inge (d. 1954), Dean of St Paul's 1911–1934, was also a prolific journalist and author. His memorial is unique in that it was 'Erected by the Publishers of his Writings'. There is a fine bust of Dean Inge in the cathedral library.

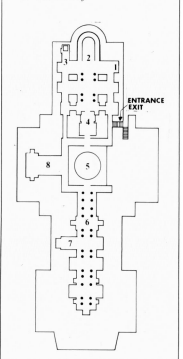

TOUR OF THE CRYPT

1 Sir Christopher Wren's tomb
2 The Chapel of the Order of the British Empire
3 St Christopher's Chapel
4 Duke of Wellington's tomb
5 Admiral Lord Nelson's tomb
6 Wren's Great Model
7 Audio-visual lecture room
8 The Treasury

FACING PAGE: *The Treasury, seen through the steel entry gates. The Crafts Council organised a design competition for these gates which was won by Alan Evans of Gloucestershire. The display case seen in the background holds the Jubilee Cope and Mitre.*

ABOVE: *The O.B.E. Chapel at the east end of the Crypt. It was designed by Lord Mottistone, Surveyor to the Fabric of St Paul's Cathedral 1957–63.*

RIGHT: *The Jubilee Cope, which was embroidered by students of the Stanhope Institute under the direction of Beryl Dean, to mark The Queen's Silver Jubilee in 1977. It was presented to the Diocese of London and is now on display in the Treasury. The decoration includes spires of London churches and the cathedral dome.*

21

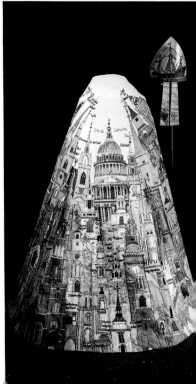

TOP LEFT: *Memorial to Florence Nightingale (1820–1910).*

TOP RIGHT: *Bust of Sir Christopher Wren (1632–1723) by Edward Pierce (Ashmolean Museum).*

ABOVE: *The tomb of Sir Christopher Wren.*

RIGHT: *This sarcophagus was originally made for Cardinal Wolsey but was not used until Admiral Nelson's death.*

Behind the Scenes

The early morning visitor to St Paul's any weekday, passing the statue of Queen Anne, will see the broad flight of steps at the west end being hosed and brushed clean after the previous day's litter of cans, wrappings and empty packets has been cleared away.

Inside, at ground-floor level, the daily round of cleaning, dusting and polishing is in its final stages. Here, and in other areas of the great cathedral, electricians, plumbers, painters and others are engaged in the unending maintenance work. At intervals throughout the day, there will be services and sessions of public prayer. All these activities, and the frequent special and national services and assemblies, involve not only faith and dedication, but also skilful organisation and administration.

St Paul's Cathedral is governed by the **Dean and Chapter**, that is to say, by the Dean, the Very Revd. Alan Webster, and the four Residentiary Canons: the Archdeacon of London; the Chancellor, the Treasurer and the Precentor, of St Paul's. The present members of the Chapter are the Ven. Frank Harvey, the Rt. Revd. Kenneth Woollcombe, the Revd. Canon K. Graham Routledge and the Revd. Prebendary P. W. Ball. Their regular, formal meetings are held in the Chapter House, which is also the Administrative centre.

Policies and programmes decided upon at Chapter meetings are carried out by the cathedral staff, under the direction of the **Registrar and Receiver**, Commander Charles Shears.

There is a tablet in the Crypt which

lists the men who have held the ancient office of **Clerk of the Works** since the destruction of Old St Paul's. The 14th name is that of the present holder, Robert Harvey. He was appointed in 1965, having served under his predecessor, Charles Linge, for six years.

With a staff of only 23 people, he is responsible for the maintenance and security, not only of the cathedral, but also the Choir School and adjoining flats, and the nine houses in Amen Court. A constant watch is kept on the state of the cathedral building by means of devices known as 'tell-tales'. Any developing cracks, shifts or other defects, are reported to the **Surveyor to the Fabric**, Robert Potter.

To this considerable work-load are added the tasks involved in the frequent special services, concerts and other functions. Further responsibilities devolve on the Clerk of the Works when national events take place at St Paul's. Preparations for these occasions include a great deal of moving and rearranging of furniture and fittings; additional seating has to be provided; television cameras must be accommodated and supplied with electrical power at numerous locations; sound-proof commentary boxes are constructed; and so on.

Two such events recently were the wedding of The Prince and Princess of Wales and the Falklands Thanksgiving Service. Both presented considerable organisational problems for the entire cathedral staff but, in

★

ABOVE LEFT: *The Dean's Virger, seen here in his ceremonial dress consisting of green gown with black chevrons, black cape-collar and white bow-tie. The staff he is holding is the 'Dean's Virger's virge'.*

ABOVE RIGHT: *The Dean of St Paul's with members of the Chapter.*

RIGHT: *A photograph taken after the re-erection in the Crypt of Wren's Great Model (seen in the background). Among those seated in the front row are the Surveyor to the Fabric (fourth from the left) and, next to him, the Clerk of the Works. The group includes tradesmen, members of the 'Heavy Gang' and others involved in the project.*

Robert Harvey's opinion, the most challenging occasion took place in 1965 – the State Funeral of Sir Winston Churchill.

The stonework of St Paul's, like that of other city buildings, suffers the decay and wear of time and weather; so, great quantities of stone have to be selected, stored, cut and shaped, to keep the cathedral in sound condition.

Down in the undercroft, which adjoins the Crypt, are the stone-yard and the masons' workshop. This is the base from which Leonard Davies, the **Master Mason**, operates. He started as a young mason at St Paul's in 1952 and gained invaluable experience working on the restoration of the north-east part of the building. The structural bomb-damage there was most severe. With the temporary roof cover removed, one could look up, as the Master Mason says, from the Crypt to the stars. This meant that there were saucer domes and lunettes, in addition to pillars and arches, to be rebuilt.

The limestone used on the outside of the building today is still Portland Stone, and from the same quarry which Wren patronised. Moreover, it is handled with the same care and skill by Leonard Davies as it was by

Wren's men, Edward and Thomas Strong, who, as their memorial declares, 'made shapely the stones of St Paul's Cathedral'.

Tony Webb has been the cathedral's **Master Carver** since 1972, but he had worked on several projects at St Paul's before that time. As an architectural sculptor (a carver in wood and stone) with the firm of Bradford of Southwark, he was involved in the stone carving in the North Transept during the mid-1950s. That was part of the repairing of bomb damage. Later, in 1963, he did the lime-wood carvings around the body of the new pulpit. Among his recent stone carvings are new urns for the South Portico.

Tony Webb's finest original wood carving to date is the aumbry door in the North Transept Chapel, which is described earlier in this guide. Yet the Master Carver's chief and continuing occupation is in restoring and repairing the carvings of Grinling Gibbons and Jonathan Maine, the two great artist-craftsmen employed by Christopher Wren. He has studied their work for over 30 years. This knowledge, and Tony Webb's own skills, ensure that his restorations blend indistinguishably with the 300-year-old carvings.

High standards of music in St Paul's were set in the 19th century by the organists Sir John Stainer and, following him, Sir George Martin. Those standards are maintained today by the present **Cathedral Organist**, Christopher Dearnley; by the members of the choir and the **Master of the Choir**.

Music is played and sung at many

★

ABOVE LEFT: *The Master of the Choir leading the boys to divine service.*

TOP: *A mason at work in the stone-yard in the undercroft. He is cutting and shaping limestone for the South Portico of the cathedral – the major restoration task begun in 1983.*

ABOVE: *The cathedral's Master Carver. He is seen here repairing and restoring some of the Grinling Gibbons decorations in the choir stalls.*

FACING PAGE: *A corner of the Library, showing some of the original bookcases on the ground floor containing leather-bound volumes bequeathed in 1713 by Bishop Compton. As can be seen, the gallery is supported by carved oak brackets. There are 32 brackets in all, and the carver, Jonathan Maine, was paid £208 for the work – that is, £6.10s for each bracket.*

hundreds of regular and special services each year. The quality of St Paul's music has been appreciated by an ever-increasing audience during recent years, through the records which the choir and the organist have made and of which there have been large sales in Britain and abroad.

The **Cathedral Choir** consists of 12 men, who are known as 'vicars-choral', and 30 boys. The boys are housed and educated in the Choir School which is situated opposite the east end of the cathedral. In their busy daily routine, these young choristers have to cope with academic studies and musical instrument practice, in addition to taking part in services and rehearsals. The **Headmaster of the Choir School**, Derek Sutton, has written: 'The choristers' life is a dedicated existence . . . most of them appear to enjoy the life, to thrive on it and to feel no sense of deprivation. It may not be too much to suggest that they develop a sense of purpose, and experience a "job satisfaction", that others may acquire much later or not at all.'

The **Library** of the Dean and Chapter of St Paul's is situated in the south-west corner of the cathedral at the Triforium level. The room itself, consisting of a ground floor and gallery lined with book presses, is a splendid example of design and craftsmanship by Wren and his associates. The fine oak parquet floor was laid by the joiner, Sir Charles Hopson. Jonathan Maine was responsible for the brackets supporting the gallery and these, in the opinion of the present Master Carver, represent the finest wood carvings in the cathedral. The stone carving on the eight pilasters is probably the work of Grinling Gibbons.

There are many rare and valuable volumes in the bookstock, nearly two thousand of which were bequeathed in 1713 by Bishop Henry Compton whose portrait hangs above the Library fireplace. Among the items unique to St Paul's, there are many manuscript volumes of church music of the 17th and 18th centuries. There is also a fully indexed collection of over 10,000 printed pamphlets.

The Library – including the chamber and the entire stock of books and other printed material – is currently being completely refurbished and, for some years, it will not be open to view. However, research scholars who need to consult particular items not available elsewhere are still received by appointment.

Throughout the hours of opening of the cathedral, there are **Virgers** on duty in all parts. (St Paul's still uses, rather than 'verger', the older spelling of the word which most dictionaries now omit or describe as 'obsolete'.) There are six Virgers and eleven Assistant-Virgers. They dress uniformly in black gowns, which are obviously appropriate, for they unfailingly attract the enquiring visitor and subdue the occasional misbehaver.

They are headed by the **Dean's Virger**, Dixon Asquith, who leads the Dean to the pulpit when he is preaching in the cathedral. He also leads the Dean in ceremonial processions, with fellow virgers preceding other dignitaries. When performing these duties, they carry their rods or 'virges', from which their name is derived. Along with several volunteers of the **Friends of St Paul's** (who may be recognised by their lapel badges) they direct visitors and answer many hundreds of questions every day. Yet the virgers' most important responsibility is towards the cathedral as a House of God. They ensure that sessions of prayer and religious services are duly respected, and that those who come to worship in St Paul's are properly received and made welcome.

The History of St Paul's

For thirteen and a half centuries a cathedral dedicated to the honour of Saint Paul has stood upon the summit of Ludgate Hill. Sir Christopher Wren's great Renaissance church which rises majestically over the City is the fifth to bear the name of London's patron saint.

The history of St Paul's begins with the consecration of Mellitus as bishop of the East Saxons by St Augustine of Canterbury in A.D 604. His cathedral, which was probably a wooden structure, was founded by Ethelbert, King of Kent, who endowed it with the Manor of Tillingham in Essex – an estate which, to this day, is still held by the Dean and Chapter.

The first cathedral was destroyed by fire – a peril which through the centuries has beset all five churches. It was rebuilt in stone in 675–685 by the saintly Bishop Erkenwald whose shrine attracted many pilgrims to the cathedral throughout the middle ages. This church was destroyed by the Vikings in the 9th century and again rebuilt in 962.

In 1087 the Saxon church was also burned down. Rebuilding, which began almost at once, had the support of William Rufus, son of William the Conqueror, whom he had just succeeded as king. Maurice, a Norman, and sometime chaplain and chancellor to William the Conqueror, had

been appointed Bishop of London the previous year. He seized the opportunity to build a cathedral on a vaster scale than anything previously envisaged in London. This cathedral, familiarly known as 'Old St Paul's', stood within spacious precincts enclosed by walls. It consisted of a nave of twelve bays, transepts and a short apsidal choir, all built in the round-arched, or Norman style. Work on the choir was delayed by a fire in 1136 and it was not in use until 1148 when the remains of St Erkenwald were translated to a new shrine behind the high altar. The cathedral was finally finished and dedicated in 1240.

As services in the cathedral became more elaborate, it was decided to pull down the Norman choir and to replace it with a larger one in the more graceful Gothic style. Work began about 1258 and was completed by 1314. The length of the building grew to 596 feet. Not only was St Paul's the largest church in England but it was surpassed in size among European cathedrals only by Seville and Milan.

The spire, 489 feet high and the loftiest that had ever been built, was completed in 1315. It was struck by lightning in 1447 and was not repaired until 1462 when the weathercock upon a ball capable of holding ten bushels of corn was reerected.

The 14th century brought great

and splendid changes to the interior of the cathedral. The floors were paved with marble and the relics of St Erkenwald, which had achieved a reputation for working miracles, were translated to another and more magnificent shrine adorned with gold. Sumptuous chantry chapels were built where Masses were offered for the souls of the founders.

During the early 15th century, St Paul's was the setting for many trials for heresy and witchcraft. The unhappy souls found guilty passed from its precincts to nearby Smithfield to die by burning at the stake.

The most famous part of the precincts in the middle ages was

★

ABOVE: *Paul's Cross. This open-air pulpit stood at the north-east corner of the precincts of Old St Paul's for over five centuries. It was a general meeting point where sermons and proclamations were delivered and trials and discussions took place. Early in the 17th century the pulpit was taken down.*

LEFT: *The medieval cathedral as it appeared before the spire was struck by lightning and burned down on 4 June 1561.*

FACING PAGE ABOVE: *Visscher's view of London in 1616 showing Old St Paul's after the spire was burned down.*

FACING PAGE BELOW: *The Great Fire of London of 1666. It started on 2 September and raged westwards across the City. The flames leaped across the cathedral precincts, setting light to scaffolding around the tower, and soon Old St Paul's was virtually reduced to ashes.*

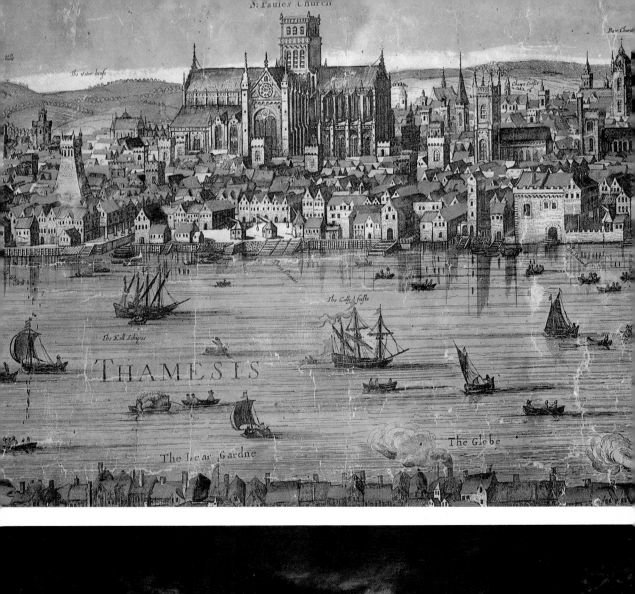

Paul's Cross, an open-air pulpit and the scene of many fiery sermons, particularly during the Reformation. To the east lay the Cathedral School which was refounded in 1512 by Dean Colet. This school – now very well known as St Paul's School – was transferred to Hammersmith in 1884 and is now in Barnes.

A state occasion of great magnificence at the beginning of the 16th century was the marriage of Arthur, Prince of Wales to Princess Catherine of Aragon, but within six months Catherine was a widow. Seven years later, quietly at Greenwich, she married her brother-in-law, Henry VIII. Henry frequently attended St Paul's on state occasions.

The reigns of Henry VIII and Edward VI saw great changes in the Church of England; at the onset of the Reformation the churches were despoiled of their wealth and treasures and the services reduced to the utmost simplicity. St Paul's suffered no less than others in this respect. On St Barnabas's Day, 1549, the high altar was pulled down and in its place a plain table, for the administration of the sacrament, was set up in the middle of the choir. The reredos was hacked to ruins and, among the tombs, only that of John of Gaunt was by royal command spared damage.

Although the old ritual and some of the former glory was restored during the five-year reign of Mary I, it was again suppressed on the accession of her half-sister, Elizabeth I. The Latin services were discontinued and the images which had been restored by Mary quietly removed at night.

Shortly after Elizabeth became queen there occurred the first calamity that led to the decay of Old St Paul's. On the afternoon of 4 June 1561, during a severe thunderstorm, the spire was again struck by lightning. In an age when lightning conductors were unknown, the spire soon caught alight and burnt downwards to the square tower and so to the roofs which were badly damaged. Although no attempt was made to re-erect the spire, the cathedral was made usable by Bishop Grindal at his own expense, and, on Sunday, 27 November 1588, Elizabeth I came to the great service of thanksgiving for victory over the Spanish armada. She was carried to the cathedral amid a blare of trumpets in a chariot 'like a throne' drawn by four white horses. The lower battlements of the cathedral were bedecked with ensigns captured from the enemy's ships.

After the Reformation, houses and shops were erected right up to the very walls of the cathedral. The old practice of using the long nave, popularly known as 'Paul's Walk', as a passageway, and of conducting business there, grew to scandalous lengths. Against a background of babble and chatter, with tradespeople selling their wares and horses being led through the building, services were held in the choir. Despite protests, this state of affairs continued until the end of the Norman cathedral. It was even revived in 1724 in the new cathedral but was finally abolished by order of Bishop Gibson.

James I took a personal interest in a project of restoration and in 1620 a Royal Commission was set up, but work did not commence until 1628 when the vigorous William Laud became bishop and Inigo Jones, the famous architect, was appointed King's Surveyor.

Jones demolished the houses and shops that had been built up against the cathedral and encased the nave in ashlar masonry with windows in the classical style in place of the medieval tracery. He altered the west front by removing the original triple Norman entrances and erected a splendid though incongruous portico in the Corinthian order surmounted by a balustrade, and attempted to strengthen and patch-up the entire fabric. This work, costing approximately £100,000, took place between 1634 and 1643, when the Civil War put a stop to building.

The Parliamentarians then appropriated the £17,000 remaining in the repair fund and, to pay their

★

FACING PAGE ABOVE: *Portrait of Sir Christopher Wren, by J. B. Closterman, in the possession of the Royal Society, London.*

FACING PAGE BELOW: *Wren's Great Model, of oak, which took nine months to make and cost over £500.*

ABOVE RIGHT: *St Paul's amid the flames during the air-raid of 29 December 1940. Although some dome timbers caught fire, no serious damage was caused.*

RIGHT: *One of the great occasions in the recent history of St Paul's was the Service of Thanksgiving on 7 June 1977 for the Silver Jubilee of Her Majesty The Queen.*

troops, sold the scaffolding – as a result of which part of the south transept collapsed. The east end of the cathedral was used by Cornelius Burgess, a puritan, as a preaching house; the nave became a cavalry barracks for the puritan soldiery; the windows were all smashed, and the carved woodwork burnt as firewood.

Thus the ravages of the Civil War completed the deterioration which had commenced with the fire of 1561 and by 1660, when Charles II was restored to the throne, St Paul's was in the final stages of decay and despoliation – 'a loathsome Golgotha' as one contemporary described it.

In 1663 another Royal Commission on St Paul's was set up. The exact date when Sir Christopher Wren was consulted is not known, but his report was issued on 1 May 1666. It is pointless to speculate on the incongruous appearance planned for St Paul's, with Inigo Jones' classical nave and Wren's proposed classical cupola joined to the Gothic choir, for the cathedral was totally destroyed in the Great Fire of London in 1666.

A complete rebuilding was now obviously essential and on 2 July 1668, Dean Sancroft wrote to Wren on behalf of the commissioners, desiring him to prepare a design for submission to the king. Thus began the plans for the fifth and present cathedral but seven years were to pass before the first stone was laid. Wren, now Surveyor-General, produced three designs.

The first, the so-called 'New Model' and the second, the 'Great Model' (now on view in the Crypt) were approved by the king but rejected by the commissioners on the ground that they were too untraditional.

Wren's third and last plan is known as the 'Warrant Design'. More traditional, it was based on the Latin cross plan, the western arm (the nave) being longer than the eastern (the choir), with a domed crossing between nave and choir. There were shallow transepts on the north and south, and a western portico. This design was accepted by the king, though acceptance was not unanimous among the commissioners. The king, a shrewd reader of men, probably understood something of the cross-currents between the architect and the commissioners and the royal warrant authorising the design in April 1675 permitted 'variations, rather ornamental than essential'.

ABOVE: *The wedding of the Prince of Wales to the Lady Diana Spencer took place in St Paul's Cathedral on* *29 July 1981. This magnificent picture shows the bride and groom at the High Altar during the service.*